ଔ

May Every Voice Sing

ଔ

ℭℜ

May Every Voice Sing

℘

Written By Dana Rondel

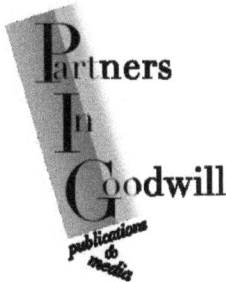

Partners **I**n **G**oodwill

publications & media

What Inspiration Sounds and Looks Like
www.partnersingoodwill.com

And, oh! The Master Mind may well
In pride of gentleness rejoice
That in the Mansions none may quell
The lilt of any nation's voice;
But every race may sing their joy,
May hymn their pride, their glories boast
To listeners glad without alloy—
The primal, well-extending host,
The founding, freedom-loving race
Whose generous-visioning mind doth see
No worth in holding foremost place,
Save in an Empire of the Free...

- **Edward William Thomson**
  The Many-Mansioned House

May the Sacred Psalms of this work
be sung by the voice of your
mind, heart and soul...
And may you live them
all your days on earth...

Make a joyful noise unto the LORD, all the earth: make a
loud noise, and rejoice, and sing praise.
Sing unto the LORD with the harp; with the harp, and the
voice of a psalm.

- Psalm 98:4-5

Any musical person who has never heard a Negro
Congregation under the spell of religious fervor sing these old
songs, has missed one of the most thrilling emotions which the
human heart may experience.

- James Weldon Johnson

May the people praise you, O God;
May all the people praise you.
Then the land will yield its harvest,
And God, our God, will bless us.

- Psalm 67:5-7

I was lucky, as many of my generation was, in having a man
like Dr. King in our lives. He came at a time that we needed to
take a long look at each other and see how similar we were.

- Lena Horne

A heart in tune with God will sing his praises...

-    *Psalm 147:1*

✳
✳
✳

Lift Every Voice and Sing

✳
✳
✳

Lift Every Voice and Sing

Lift ev'ry voice and sing,
Till earth and heaven ring,
Ring with the harmonies of Liberty;
Let our rejoicing rise
High as the list'ning skies,
Let it resound loud as the rolling sea.
Sing a song full of the faith that the dark past has taught us,
Sing a song full of the hope that the present has brought us;
Facing the rising sun of our new day begun,
Let us march on till victory is won...

✳

✳

✳

America

✳

✳

✳

America

America is a land full of hope and promise. Its fertile soil, which holds within it God's dreams, has birthed for our souls rich harmonies and for our eyes splendid realities. These sundry tones and hues of life make for the beauty that our seasons bring. In New England, this beauty encompasses the inner reflections and nudeness of creation in winter, the burgeoning of a new world in spring, Nature's full blossom in summer, and autumn becomes a time for us to simply remember that all things were possible, so let us continue to march on...

It has often been said, in order to know our future we must understand our past; therefore, in each of our days, as we're journeying toward tomorrow, it is necessary for us, all of humanity, to carry and nurture within ourselves, like the season of winter, the raw seed of inspiration that beckons to be born into something more than what it was yesterday. What was hope then, in those days before? Does America have a story? I believe she does...

✳
✳
✳

Lift Every Voice and Sing

✳
✳
✳

Lift Every Voice and Sing

Stony the road we trod,
Bitter the chast'ning rod,
Felt in the days when hope unborn had died;
Yet with a steady beat, have not our weary feet
Come to the place for which our fathers sighed?
We have come over a way that with tears has been watered.
We have come, treading our path through the blood of the
slaughtered, out from the gloomy past,
Till now we stand at last
Where the white gleam of our bright star is cast.

✳
✳
✳

Her History

✳
✳
✳

Her History

America, part of her history is black. Every story before it is born must experience its time in the dark and fertile womb of life. Here is where the first tune of creation is felt. Where a sound by itself renders a musical note so full of harmony that a rainbow has only to show itself in one color; yet what is a story if it has only one note, one color? What song will it sing? The season of winter must share her dream and allow us to witness not only her potential, but ours too.

✳
✳
✳

Lift Every Voice and Sing

✳
✳
✳

Lift Every Voice and Sing

God of our weary years,
God of our silent tears,
Thou who hast brought us thus far on the way;
Thou who hast by Thy might,
Led us into the light,
Keep us forever in the path, we pray.
Lest our feet stray from the places, our God,
where we met Thee,
Lest our hearts, drunk with the wine of the world,
we forget Thee;
Shadowed beneath Thy hand,
May we forever stand,
True to our God,
True to our native land.

✳
✳
✳

A New Day

✳
✳
✳

A New Day

Winter again brought forth a new day, and spring was born so she could rise and reveal for us her iridescent hues of light. Now there is a song to be sung and a story to be told. Men, women and children, native to this land and who were brought here from Africa and other places abroad, forced into mental, emotional and physical bondage, wanted us, the world, to hear their music, whether motivated by laughter or tears, see their words, whether inspired by joy or pain, and affirm with our lives the worth and value of their creative designs, whether influenced by the rays of freedom or murky clouds of slavery. These souls, once subjected, wanted to know why their voices had to remain silenced; why the veil of ignorance had to remain over their eyes, and why their able hands and feet had to remain fettered and still. "How long before spring would come?" they had often asked. "Aren't we a part of America too?"

✳
✳
✳

Look Back

✳
✳
✳

Look Back

Aren't we a part of America too? Who, besides those of us who call ourselves black, hasn't asked this question? Even if these words were only a passing thought or a silent utterance, they were once explored by every American: red, white, yellow and black, for each of us have at one time or another felt a sense of displacement in this land. And America, on many occasions, has answered by impelling us all to look back. Her story is ours. Ours, too, is hers. They are one story which acknowledges that all of our history is at first black, for all thought, ideas and dreams had to be nurtured in darkness, creation's womb, before they were born into a world where they could be heard, seen and experienced.

✷
✷
✷

Black History

✷
✷
✷

Black History

Black History is the past bringing itself forward in order for America to learn more of who she is. Her children are those who have made sweet sounding music and lifted their voices to sing even when it was hard to; they are those who painted themselves brown and black, yet knew they were every color of the rainbow; they are those who molded, shaped and built the treasures, landscapes and foundations of earth, first with their words, then with their hands and feet, whether or not external time favored them. The children of America and of our Black History are simply those who have let themselves die, be reborn and rise again...And in some way they have learned to tell their story. And America has learned to listen.

✳
✳
✳

Rise Again

✳
✳
✳

.

Rise Again

Rise again....So like our ancestors, enslaved and free, he, Barack Obama, has and so must we. Sons and daughters of this blessed land, America, and of all the earth, let us now recognize our brother who urges us not to keep our heads looking only back, for although winter has held and nurtured our dreams and spring has given them life, summer, too, wants to fulfill her promise. We, along with our friend and President of the United States, know that it is time to give hope its wings and let it fly. The light of our land is not only for a few, nor is it only for America's children, but it is for all of those who are ready to shine and let their light come forth. The earth calls to us and says, yes, your history is black and beautiful, recognize it as such, and yes, it, too, is colorful and bright, therefore, you must cherish it in all of its glory. And in doing so, may we forever stand together true to our God, true to ourselves and true to our native lands....

The Wall defendeth all alike,
The Master Mind on all ordains:—
Within my bound no sword shall strike,
Nor fetter bind, save law arraigns;
No prisoner here shall feel the rack,
No infant be to slavery born,
The wage shall labor's sweat not lack,
Nor skill of just reward be shorn.
The king and hind alike shall stand
Within the peril of my law,
And though it change at time's demand
Shall every change be held in awe.
Here every voice may freely speak
Wisdom or folly as it choose,
And though the strong must lead the weak,
The weak may yet the strong refuse;
Thus shall no change be wrought before
The wise who seek a better way
Can win, to share their vision, more
Than praise the wise who wish delay—
That so the Master Mind be strong
Through every drift of time and change,
To fashion either right or wrong
At will, within the mansion's range.

- **Edward William Thomson**
  The Many-Mansioned House

Be still and know that I am God. I will be exalted among the nations. I will be exalted in the earth.

- Psalm 46:10

Oh, God of Dust and Rainbows,
Help us to see
That without the dust the rainbow
Would not be.

- Langston Hughes

The Lord looks down from heaven on the human race to see if there are any who understand, any who seek God.

- Psalm 14:2

While others fight for power
We can walk among the flowers
Knowing that the best thing in life
Is the thing that is free
Love for you and me...Love is still king,
Love is the thing...

- Lena Horne

Being a singer is a natural gift. It means I'm using to the highest degree possible the gift that God gave me to use...

- Aretha Franklin

The original writings by the author of this book were inspired by James Weldon Johnson's hymn: "Lift Every Voice and Sing," the many contributions made by "Blacks" or "African Americans," to grow this country we call "America," in spite of their hardships, namely slavery, racism and sexism, and the election of Barack Obama, President of the United States.

<u>Omniversal Life International (OLI) Life and Leadership</u>

Omniversal Life International (OLI) provides the necessary training, tools and wisdom to become a wiser and happier individual as well as a renowned leader in the professional world. Our leaders, those who have been trained within the OLI Life & Leadership Program, have the capacity to guide others toward outcomes that allow for healthier relationships, greater personal and professional growth and higher tangible returns. What makes *Omniversal Life International (OLI)* different? Our Life & Leadership Program is based on spiritual principles that are universal and effective.

Like *Wisdom In New Dimensions (WIND)*, we want you and/or your organization to greatly benefit from the invaluable insight gained through the OLI Life & Leadership Program, therefore we would like you to visit our web site and learn more about us:

www.windinc.org

Partners In Goodwill

Publications & Media

What Inspiration Sounds and Looks Like.

Books, Music, Multi-Media, Creative Print Designs,
Writing and Publishing

www.partnersingoodwill.com

Public Speaking & Book Signings

www.danarondel.com

The Book of Psalms

❧

And those who know thy name
Will put their trust in Thee;
For Thou, O Lord, has not
Forsaken those who seek Thee.

-     Psalm 9:10

☙

You are the instrument in which God's breath flows through. What music will I hear? My soul is lifted only by harmony, so write me a song that will make me rise...

-   Dana Rondel

◆

◆

◆

◆

◆

◆

◆

◆

◆

◆

◆

◆

◆

◆

◆

◆

◆

◆

◆

◆

◆

◆

◆

◆

◆

◆

◆

◈

◆

◆

◆

◆

www.ingramcontent.com/pod-product-compliance
Lightning Source LLC
Chambersburg PA
CBHW020508100426
42813CB00030B/3164/J